THE PRAYING CHILD

THE PRAYING CHILD

Every Child is Unique and Special

Simi Bello

Copyright © 2022 by Simi Bello

All rights reserved. No part of this book may be reproduced or used in any manner without written permission of the copyright owner except for the use of quotations in a book review.

FIRST EDITION

978-1-80227-679-4 (paperback)
978-1-80227-646-6 (ebook)

I love children and believe that every child should have the right foundation, which will go a long way to help them in life. Children need to learn how to control their emotions early in life, speak out when something is not right but also be able to pray for other people, look out for them, listen and care for them just as God cares for us.

YOU ARE NOT ALONE

You are a unique child created to do great things in life.

Some things might be happening around you that you do not understand.

It might be at home, school, church, a friend's place or other places.

The most important thing you should never forget is that you are not alone.

It is good to be honest always; that is the right thing to do. Mum, dad, teachers or friends might have told lies and got away with it, but it is not right.

Remember to stay honest because it is the right thing to do.

You might be punished for speaking the truth sometimes, but it is still the right thing to do.

Do you wish mum, dad or some of your friends could be more caring sometimes?

Do you wish you had a different dad, mum, teacher or even friends? You are not alone; some other children feel the same way too. Mum, dad, teachers or friends may not always get it right. We must love them regardless. That's what makes us humans.

Have you ever felt that some people are not friendly to you? Do you think some people do not want to play with you at school, home or places you go? It sometimes happens to adults too. Give them some time, and they will come around. But that should not stop you from being nice to everyone around you, especially those you think are not nice to you.

JESUS CARES

You must know that one person knows how you feel, especially when sad or afraid.

He is always honest, never wrong, and loves you more than anyone. He is Jesus; you can always talk to Him in prayer.

BE POLITE

Do not forget to be polite. Always use the magic words "please" and "thank you." It is the right thing to do. Some adults or even your classmates might not be polite. But remember, it does not make it right. Being polite will take you far in life.

FEAR

Have you ever been afraid of anything? You are not alone. Some adults still get scared sometimes. But remember, Jesus loves you. He will protect you.

You can be that person everyone wants to be like, and even some adults would wish they could be like you. You can be better by listening to your teachers at school and obeying dad and mum always, even when it seems hard. Playing nicely with those around you both at school and home. Being friendly at all times; be that friend everyone wants to play with always.

You can be that praying child who prays for mum, dad, teachers and even friends. When you pray, Jesus will answer you, which will make you very happy.

The people you think are not friendly to you might become your good friends. Mum and dad would turn out to be the best parents. That is what your prayer can do. Remember, you can learn to pray about anything and everything.

Be Blessed!

www.ingramcontent.com/pod-product-compliance
Lightning Source LLC
Chambersburg PA
CBHW042107090526
44590CB00004B/131